JAMES ARTHUR

My story

JAMES ARTHUR

My story

THE OFFICIAL  WINNER'S BOOK

Photography by Ken McKay

HarperCollins*Publishers*

NICOLE ON JAMES

Guys, thank you so much for all the incredible support you gave James during the competition. I loved working with him week after week and seeing how he could take a song, totally turn it on its head and 'James Arthur' it. He truly is an incredible artist and a real one-off and I am so excited to see what his future holds!

Nicole Scherzinger, December 2012

#1 STARTING OUT

IN THE BEGINNING . . .

I was born James Andrew Arthur in Redcar, Middlesbrough, on 2 March 1988. My parents, Shirley and Neil, split up when I was very young and I stayed in Redcar with my mum. I was a normal little boy who liked running around with my mates, playing and getting into trouble.

If I am being honest I don't think I was the easiest child to look after. I was very naughty and I think people around me thought I suffered from attention deficit hyperactivity disorder because of the way I acted. I don't know if I actually had ADHD because I was never tested, but let's just say that I was quite 'spirited'. I was always messing about and getting told off. It was nothing really bad, just the usual kids' stuff.

I first started singing when I was about six. I'd literally sing along to whatever my mum was playing on her CD player and people always said I was really good. I was more into running about like a headless chicken at that time, so I certainly didn't think about singing as a

LEFT / I first got into music when I was about six years old, just singing (and strumming) along to whatever my mum was playing.   **17**

career. I didn't think about anything as a career – I was all about having fun and scoring goals.

Both of my parents were massively into music when I was growing up. My mum always played a lot of Michael Jackson and David Bowie, and when I was with my dad I'd hear loads of heavy metal like Black Sabbath, AC/DC and Led Zeppelin. My music upbringing was pretty eclectic in terms of the variety of what I listened to. That's given me an appreciation of all kinds of music, so I'm really grateful to my parents for that.

I don't think it will come as a massive shock to anyone to hear that I wasn't the greatest at school. I really liked P.E. because I got to play games, and I was pretty good at English. I always picked up language quite well, so I loved creative writing. I'd often write little stories and I had a good imagination. I was terrible at maths, though. I used to daydream my way through the lessons and I couldn't get the hang of it at all. I didn't see the point in trying to do something I wasn't good at. I've always been a bit like that. I only like doing things I can do really well in.

I've got one brother, Neil, who's 34, and four sisters: Sian, who's 26, Charlotte, 18, Jasmine, 18, and Neve, who's 12, and they're all lovely. Because Neve is still quite young I didn't live with her for very long before I left home, but we're incredibly close. Sian and I were either thick as thieves or fighting like cat and dog when we were younger. We used to conjure up little plans together all the time. When we were left alone with a babysitter we used to make fake sick, using things we found in the bathroom. We'd pretend one of us was ill so we could go downstairs and watch TV instead of going to bed.

When I was about four or five we were bouncing around on the sofa in our living room and I fell off and crashed into a glass-topped table. I cut my eye on the corner of the table and I got rushed to hospital. It turned out I had severed some of my nerves, and as a result I got a lazy eye. I had it corrected, but even to this day I've got a complex about my eye turning in when I'm talking to people. I find it hard to keep eye contact because I'm so self-conscious about it. That's one of my earliest memories, and it's quite a dramatic one.

From a really young age I was best friends with a boy called Michael Dawson, and we're still best mates now. Two other friends called Callum and Dean lived on my street, and I used to play with them all the time too. We were lucky because we had a park directly opposite our house, and we were always in there mucking about. When I make friends I tend to stick with them, and I'm very loyal.

My mum remarried when I was nine, and we all moved to Bahrain because her new husband got a job out there. It was a complete contrast to the life I was living before in every way, but it was great being exposed to something so different at such a young age. I especially liked school as all the kids in my class were from all over the world, so I experienced a lot of different cultures. In Bahrain we had a much grander lifestyle than the one I had been used to, so it was a bit of a culture shock at first.

None of my mates sang or performed when I was growing up, and I didn't really tell anyone that I did it on the quiet. When I first realised that I wanted to be a singer I kept it to myself, and it wasn't until I moved to Bahrain that I even took part in a school performance.

When I was about 12 or 13 they gave me the part of the undertaker in the musical *Oliver!* I also played the General in *The Pirates of Penzance*. I won the Performance of the Year award from my school for my role as the General. All my family and friends said how good I was in the role. At the time I just thought they were being nice because I was young, and I didn't realise I had any proper talent. Whenever I was in plays it was because my teachers used to encourage me to get involved, and they really pushed me, otherwise I'm not sure I would have bothered.

I had a lot more confidence back then, so I just used to dive in without thinking. I was a bit of a loudmouth, I didn't take any crap from anybody, and I was pretty laid-back and happy.

We stayed in Bahrain for a few years and I had an amazing time. We came back down to earth with a bit of a bump when my mum and my stepdad got divorced and all the family decided to move back to England. I guess it was a rags-to-riches, then back-to-rags kind of tale. It was once we moved back to Redcar that things began to go a bit wrong.

I started going to a local school which was quite rough. Singing and dancing weren't really the done thing. I probably would have got my head shoved down the toilet if I'd got up on stage and started singing and dancing. I stopped having anything to do with singing and I became the class clown instead!

I found it hard coming back to the same place I'd previously lived after being away for a few years. A lot had changed, and although I was able to go back to being mates with the guys I knew before, life

RIGHT / I formed my first band with some other local lads when I was 16 years old. We did quite a lot of gigs together in the area and built up a good reputation, but we never had the money to take it further.

had moved on and I didn't feel like I fitted in any more. I felt like a real outsider. I was never the guy that the girls fancied or the clever one that people looked up to, so I created this character for myself – as the joker who didn't care about anything.

Things weren't that great at home and I was arguing with my family a lot. That meant not always paying attention and basically being quite disruptive at school. I used to walk into some classes and get chucked out before I'd even had a chance to sit down. Teachers would say things like, 'I can't deal with you – you're doing my head in. Get out!'

I spent a lot of time tapping on desks and winding the teachers up. If I was asked to stop I'd do it even louder and put on some stupid accent. I secretly had it in my head by that point that I was going to be a professional singer, so I felt like school didn't matter any more.

I was really into soul and post-hardcore heavy rock music, and Nirvana were my heroes! I was also really into rappers like Eminem, because he used to sing about having a rubbish life, which I felt like I did at the time. I suppose if you were to sum up my musical tastes from when I was 14, you could say I was mainly into angry music.

In the same way as I did at school, I caused trouble at home, so my mum kicked me out quite regularly – and I can't say I blame her; I was unbearable to live with. She couldn't really cope with me and I ended up in foster care for my last year of school. That was actually my decision to a certain extent. I couldn't bear the rows at home and I hated seeing how much my behaviour hurt my mum, but I didn't seem to be able to stop myself. I was angry about everything and so I lashed out verbally. I wanted to get away from everything, and so when foster care was offered I took it. I didn't feel like I wanted to be around my mum, and she was finding me hard to handle, so it seemed like the right decision all round.

Even though I was in touch with my dad I didn't go round to see him that often, so I didn't really have a male role model during those years. I think that was part of my problem. I suppose I sometimes took on the male role in the house myself, because much of the time it was all women, and I found that quite a lot of pressure.

I was in foster care for about two years in total, until I was 17. I didn't want any of my friends at school to know that I was living in foster care, so I kept it a secret from them. If we were walking home and my mates asked me where I was going I'd lie and say I was going to stay with my auntie or something. I didn't want anyone to know the truth. It was really awkward.

When I was about 15 I decided that I wanted to learn guitar and start taking music a bit more seriously. My mum's boyfriend at the time bought me a charity shop guitar for Christmas and that was it for me. I think it cost about £40 or £50, so it wasn't the world's greatest guitar, but I loved it. I don't have it any more and I've got no idea where it's ended up but I'm keeping an eye out on eBay!

I taught myself to play and started writing songs about girls and heartbreak and all the kinds of things you go through when you're a teenager. That coincided with me having my first proper girlfriend. I was madly in love with her – or I thought I was at that age. We dated for around a year and that was my first serious relationship. I'd had other girlfriends before but that was more about sending Valentine's

cards and holding hands than anything else. I always loved women when I was growing up. I even used to flirt with my mum's friends, and I'm still the same now.

When I was young and confused by what was going on in my life, music was a coping mechanism for me. It was my escape when everything else around me was rubbish. It was my own little made-up world that I could go into. It was also a way to channel all my emotions and express how I was feeling when I didn't feel like I could do it in everyday life.

I came up with a lot of melodies. Thinking back, I'd always been humming little melodies to myself and singing tunes even when I was a kid, so it was a natural progression to put words to them. My voice wasn't great back then, to be honest. I used to listen to albums by the bands I loved and the lead singers had husky voices, so I was always trying to emulate them. That's when I started experimenting with how my voice sounds and finding out where I felt comfortable musically.

As I got more confident I slowly started to tell my friends about my singing, and surprisingly they were really interested in it all. They used to come round to my house and listen to me playing for hours. They were always saying that my lyrics were great and they encouraged me to carry on writing. I've written literally hundreds of songs now. I'm not sure how many of them will see the light of day, but hopefully one day some of them will end up on an album.

It wasn't until I left school that I really started focusing on music as a possible career. At school I was too busy messing about to think too

LEFT / I've got five siblings and we're all really close. Needless to say, when we were growing up, we got into all sorts of mischief!

far into the future, but once I had the space to decide what I wanted to do, music was really the only thing I felt passionate about.

I took all of my GCSE exams and I did okay. I got a B in English, and that was the most important subject to me, so I was really happy with that. I honestly can't remember now how many passes I got in total, but I know it wasn't many because I didn't put much effort in. I truanted quite a lot back then, and I was caught smoking in town a few times when I should have been in lessons.

After school I went to do a music course at a local college, where I learnt about the theory side of things, and we would get put into bands with other people on the course, which was a good introduction to making music with other people.

It was a two-year course, but I dropped out after a year because I felt the tutors didn't really care whether I did my work, or if I was going to make something of myself. Half the time the tutors wouldn't turn up to lessons, and sometimes I couldn't afford to pay the travel costs just to get in there, so all in all it was a bit of a disaster.

I decided that I would be better off doing things on my own, so I carried on writing and singing in my own time. I was about 16 when I formed my first band with some other local lads. We were called Traceless and we played quite a few gigs together. We supported Bromheads Jacket – they were quite big at the time – and I think we were pretty good. I remember playing a place called the Ku Bar in Stockton, and that was really special to me because I knew that the Arctic Monkeys had played it the week before. We made a name for ourselves around the local area and built up a good reputation, but

26   **RIGHT** / I played a few gigs with other bands and we did pretty well, but gradually I started getting more paid gigs as a solo artist.

we never really had the money to travel and take it further. We made it as far as Glasgow for one gig, which was great because I've got family there, so I got to see them. We really wanted to do gigs all around the country, but small gigs don't pay enough for you to be able to afford a car to travel in, let alone somewhere to stay the night.

I also did some solo gigs around the same time that I got paid for, which kept me in food and clothes. It also meant that I could just about get by living on my own from the age of 17, so I moved out of foster care and into a little flat.

The first place I lived in didn't work out – I got kicked out for partying too much – so I started staying with my friends or back with my parents until I managed to find somewhere new. There were a few times when I found myself with nowhere to live, but I was too embarrassed to tell people, so I ended up sleeping rough. It was something I had to do to survive, so I just got on with it. I feel like a lot of my younger years were about survival. It wasn't fun and I wouldn't ever want to do it again, but sometimes you have no choice and you have to do what you can to get by. As long as I had somewhere to lay my head down I didn't care.

At my lowest point I would look at pictures of my sisters and want to be around them so badly. It was really hard not being able to see them as much as I wanted to, but equally I knew I'd brought a lot of it on myself.

I stayed in touch with my family to some degree all of the time I was living away from home. I still went back to my mum's house, and stayed on occasion, but I always felt very disconnected from them. I felt like the black sheep of the family and as if I'd really let them down. They did try to reach out and help me but I wasn't in the right frame of mind to accept it. I felt like I could do everything on my own and that I was a real grown-up supporting myself.

I remember always feeling I had to prove myself to my family, so whenever I saw them I would tell them I'd got so-and-so coming up and that this amazing thing was happening with my music. Then when it didn't work out I would feel so embarrassed I didn't even want to go and see them, but I'd have no choice other than to go home with my tail between my legs and ask them to help me out with money. They didn't really have any money themselves, so I hated doing that, and I only ever did it if things got really desperate.

When Traceless split up I joined another band called Heroes and Hand Grenades, and we later changed our name to Save Arcade. We were actually really good and very successful locally, but for various reasons we eventually split up.

A few of us stayed together and formed another band called The Emerald Sky. We only got a few gigs as a band but I ended up getting more and more as a solo artist. If I managed to do a few gigs a month earning £150 a night by playing a series of covers, that would see me through financially. I'd built up a good reputation around the local area. The more people heard me and liked me, the more gigs I did, and eventually I was able to start performing my own tracks as well as covers.

A guy called Rich, who had a recording studio nearby, heard some of my music and he loved it, so he let me do recordings for free. That meant I had CDs to sell at my gigs. He suggested that I create The

James Arthur Band, which is what I went on to do. That was more of a soulful, hip-hoppy band and it was more the kind of sound I wanted to do. He offered to try and get me some gigs and it all took off.

He knew I had some sort of gift and he wanted to help me out, so he put my music out on the internet for me and promoted it. We recorded a couple of EPs and we were really hoping to get some kind of record deal. It never quite came off, and I always felt like I was heading in the right direction but not really getting where I wanted to be. It was so frustrating.

Apart from playing music I didn't really have any jobs I enjoyed when I was growing up. For a while I worked in a call centre, which I hated, then in an office, writing CVs for people, and I was always good at selling things. They were all dead-end jobs and just a way to get by really.

The thing with singing is that it's so hard to break into. If I wanted to get a job in a call centre I would see the ad, apply and then hopefully get the job, but there's nowhere you can actually apply for a job as a singer, so I did get a bit disheartened. In the back of my mind I did always feel that one day I was just going to walk into somewhere and magically someone would give me a break and I'd become famous, so I tried not to let it get me down. I felt I had a talent and I could go somewhere, so it was frustrating when things didn't work out like that straight away.

When I turned 23 I reached a point where everything seemed to be going wrong in my life and I knew that I had to go back to the root of my problems and try and fix everything. I'd had strained relationships with my parents for some time, but I was getting older and I really didn't want it to be like that any more. I needed to ask them some questions – and to apologise.

It took a lot of sitting down and talking but we got there in the end, and getting everything out made me feel more secure and stable. I found out stuff about my childhood that I hadn't known, and I got the chance to ask about my parents' break-up and all the things I had wondered about for so long. It helped to release all of the feelings I'd kept inside me for so long. Once I understood everything it made it a lot easier to deal with.

It's amazing how good it can feel saying sorry to someone. I apologised for the way I'd acted at different points over the years and it felt amazing. It also gives you the chance to put an end to a chapter of your life you're not happy with and move on.

Before I applied for *The X Factor* I was spending a lot of time in bed feeling low. I was happy that everything was back on track with my family, but music-wise things felt a bit hopeless. I didn't think I was ever going to get anywhere, even though I was working really hard. People kept telling me I was going to be a massive success, but you need that break to get your foot in the door.

I kept getting texts from friends saying, '*The X Factor* is coming. If you don't enter we're going to fall out with you,' and they really got me thinking. I had never imagined trying out for the show because I didn't feel like I would fit the criteria. I didn't think I had the right sound or look. I thought it was all about being clean cut and having a cheery sound, and that just wasn't me. The more I thought about it, though, the more I thought, 'Come on, what have I got to lose?'

#2
THE
X FACTOR
DREAM

AUDITION

After getting all the text messages encouraging me to enter *The X Factor* I decided to bite the bullet and go for it! I was very much in two minds because I thought they'd take one look at me and go, 'Nah, he doesn't look the part and he's not pop star material.'

People used to joke around and instead of saying, 'Why don't you enter *The X Factor*?' they would say, 'Why don't you go and win *The X Factor*?' People thought I was that good, and if they had that faith in me, I knew I should as well.

You can't go into the country's biggest talent show doubting yourself. I didn't want to waste my time and I was feeling very insecure about it all. Even when I looked up the audition details online I still wasn't 100 per cent certain it was for me, so I had to have a bit of a word with myself about it.

Surprisingly I wasn't that nervous on the morning of the audition. It wasn't far from where I lived, so I just stuck on some skinny jeans, a jumper and some trainers and I was good to go. I went round and borrowed £10 from my mum, got on a train on my own and then I was there.

The Middlesbrough audition was like a pre-audition with the producers, to decide whether or not I was going to get through to the judges' round, so I didn't feel as much pressure as I would have done if I'd leapt straight into singing in front of Gary Barlow!

I sang one of my own songs called 'Habit', and also 'Fallin'', by Alicia Keys. I got put through and I felt really happy when I was invited to sing for the judges in Newcastle – that's when I got properly nervous.

I didn't get much sleep at all the night before, so I wasn't feeling my best. I took all of my family and some friends along with me that time, because I really wanted the support. We all drove up there early and it was surreal seeing everyone queuing up and seeing *The X Factor* logo staring back at me everywhere I looked – that suddenly made it all seem like it was really happening!

I felt confident in my abilities, but I still wasn't feeling good about the way I looked. Having people I knew there to reassure me was a help, and it was also the extra pressure I needed to push me to do my best.

I felt sick with nerves while I was waiting to be seen. It was such a long day and it was really hot. We were all sat outside and Dermot came over to talk to me and that was so strange. He asked if I had my family with me and before he'd even finished the sentence my mum shouted, 'I'm his mum!' When she said she was very proud of me I was so chuffed. That meant so much to me.

Then my dad chipped in as well. It was amazing to have both of my parents there, because they didn't have any kind of relationship when I was growing up. They hadn't spoken properly for about 20 years, but in the days leading up to my audition they both said that they'd decided to put things behind them and move on. They both wanted to be there that day and unless they made their peace with each other that would have been impossible. They too needed to be able to move on, and as a result we were all together as a family for the first time since … well, since I can remember.

THAT DAY WAS REALLY SPECIAL FOR ME IN SO MANY WAYS AND, EVEN IF NOTHING HAD COME OF IT MUSICALLY, IT CHANGED MY LIFE FOREVER.

All of us were waiting backstage when a researcher came and told me it was my turn to perform. He took me to the side of the stage, and I saw the girl who went in front of me come off looking disheartened after getting four nos. I didn't think that was a great sign, to be honest. All I could do was go out there and do my best and hope and pray they liked me.

It was very strange going out on stage. I was used to singing to a few dozen people in pubs and clubs! Suddenly there was this nice, shiny stage and all these bright lights waiting to greet me. I looked out and I got this strange feeling in my stomach thinking, 'What the hell am I doing?' I also remember thinking that Tulisa and Nicole were gorgeous and then telling myself to concentrate on what I was there to do. Nicole asked me my name and who was with me. I told her that I had my mum and dad there, who don't usually speak to each other.

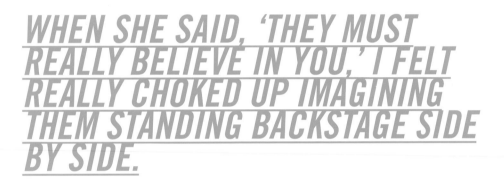

WHEN SHE SAID, 'THEY MUST REALLY BELIEVE IN YOU,' I FELT REALLY CHOKED UP IMAGINING THEM STANDING BACKSTAGE SIDE BY SIDE.

Gorgeous women aside, I had all of these panicky thoughts running through my head. I knew that so much rested on that moment. I kept thinking, 'What if they hate me? What if I get booed? What if I don't get through and then I feel stupid in front of everyone?' I felt really overwhelmed by the amount of people that were there. The noise was incredible.

Someone brought my guitar on stage for me and I performed Tulisa's 'Young'. Gary asked Tulisa if she'd ever heard anyone do an acoustic version of the track before and she said no, so at least it was

LEFT / Stepping out onto that stage with all the bright lights and the noise of the crowd was overwhelming, but having both my parents there to support me made all the difference.

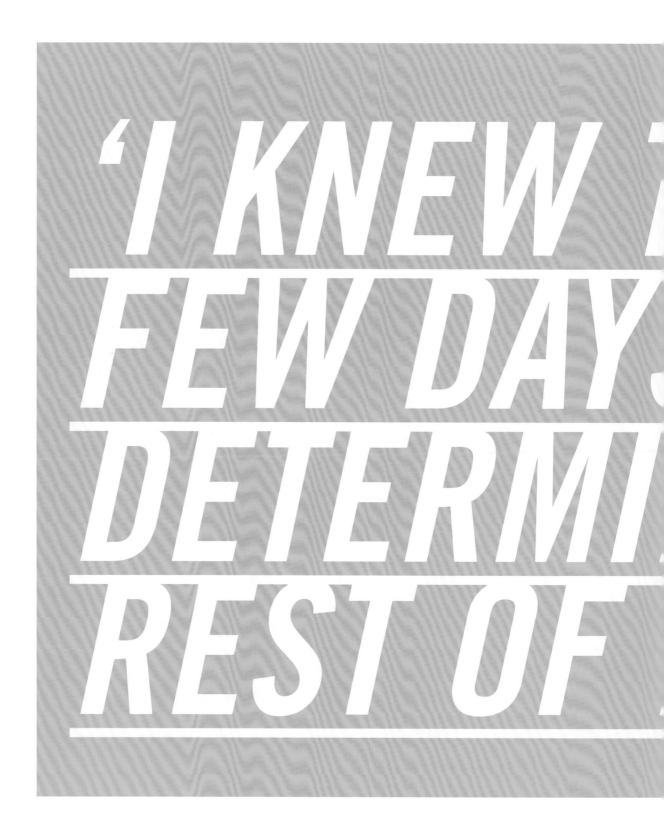
'I KNEW T
FEW DAY:
DETERMI
REST OF

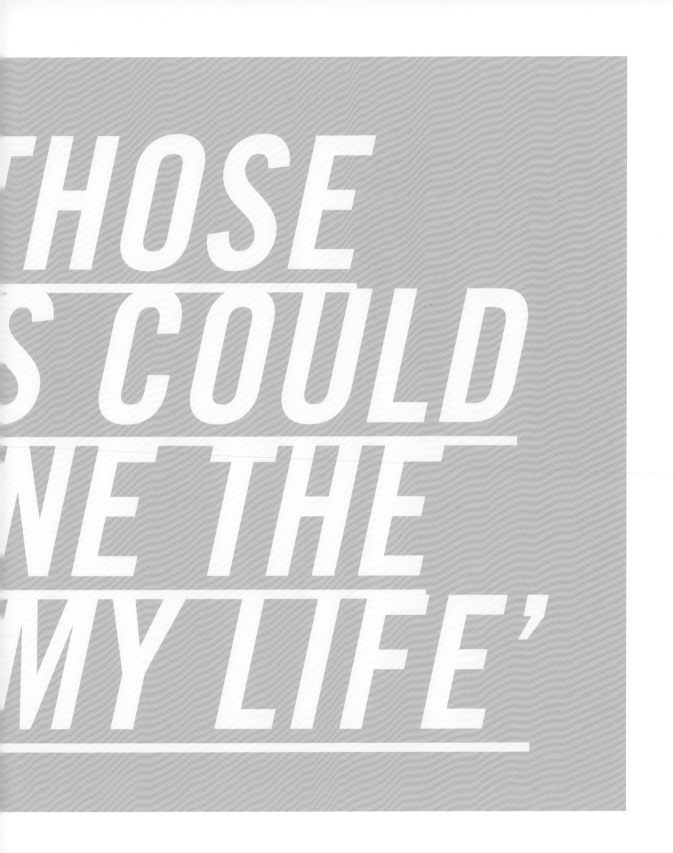

something fresh and new and I was pleased that I'd chosen it. I'd been through a lot of songs before I decided on that one, but it felt right.

Obviously I was quite nervous about singing a Tulisa song in front of her, but it was a risk I wanted to take. Tulisa had been through a bit of a tough year and so had I, so I thought she'd like it. I decided that I could tell my story through it. When I was singing that song I felt like I was asking for forgiveness from anyone I've ever hurt. I wanted a better life, which was a big part of the reason I entered the competition, and that's what I was thinking about when I was up there in front of the audience.

I was so happy when the audience cheered me about ten seconds into my song. I fed off that energy. I loved performing it so much. It was such a rush, and when I finished I let out a massive sigh of relief and started pacing the stage to keep myself from leaping around. I felt really teary when the audience stood up and started clapping me. I was trying so hard not to cry.

When I finished I had to wait for the judges' verdict, and that was definitely the scariest bit. I'd seen them smiling while I was singing, but that could mean anything. Tulisa was the first to give me feedback and she said, 'James, when you were up there I could see you get lost in that world and it's just you, the microphone and the guitar. Best audition of the day.'

Gary went next and I was waiting for him to say he didn't get it, but he said that usually when he sees people he wants to change them, but he would be angry if anyone tried to change me because I'm so good. The tears were literally bursting out of me by then!

Louis said to me that he thought my life was about to totally change and Nicole said she could understand why my mum and dad managed to put their differences aside to come along with me. Nicole said she went on the show to find an artist to inspire her, and I had. I really bared my soul that day and she totally picked up on that and said such lovely things. I knew in that moment I would really love to work with her in the future if I could.

I WAS ELATED WHEN THE JUDGES GAVE ME FOUR YESES. I JUST THOUGHT, 'BRILLIANT, I MIGHT ACTUALLY GET SOMEWHERE WITH THIS MUSIC STUFF NOW.'

It felt incredible. I was so proud of myself for getting up there and doing it and overcoming my fears. It meant the world to me and I told them as much. I was getting proper shivers, and my head was aching because I was trying so hard not to cry, but it was still the best feeling ever.

My friends and family were all waiting backstage for me and when I walked off they all ran up and hugged me and told me they knew I could do it. Everyone was in tears, and when I hugged my mum and dad at the same time it all felt like a bit of a dream. That was a really defining moment in my life.

I did a few interviews afterwards, and that's when it started to feel real – that I could actually go far in the competition. I think it was only when I got home and sat down that it totally hit me. It felt like the entire day had been a blur.

Some of my friends looked on Twitter and people who had been at the Newcastle auditions that day were already talking about me. It was a massive shock to the system that people knew who I was already. It made me realise that if I got through the next couple of rounds to the Live Shows, things could go really crazy.

I spent the time before Bootcamp seeing everyone back home and mentally preparing myself. So much of my future rested on those few days, and I wanted to make sure that I was feeling good and my voice was the best it could possibly be. I didn't buy any new clothes or anything because I couldn't afford them, so it was just a case of getting my head into the right space.

I rehearsed a lot with my band and we were still talking about trying to get a record deal. For all I knew I could have been sent home on the first day of Bootcamp, so I didn't want to chuck in the band and have nothing to come back to. Nothing was guaranteed, so I tried to get on with my everyday life as best I could. I wanted to make sure everything was still there for me if the show didn't work out.

It felt very strange sitting in my bedsit strumming on my guitar and having this ray of hope that my future could be incredibly exciting. The place I was living in wasn't exactly The Ritz, and I wanted more. I knew those few days could determine the rest of my life, turning everything from miserable to magical.

BOOTCAMP

While it was lovely that everyone around me had been so enthusiastic about me going to Bootcamp, telling me I was going to do well, I was determined to keep my feet on the ground. I've been let down a lot over the years, so I've learnt never to expect anything. Bootcamp would be a few very important days in my life, I told myself, but if I didn't get through to Judges' Houses, I would find another way to make it.

I travelled to Liverpool the night before Bootcamp kicked off, and all of the contestants were put up in a hotel together. I was sharing a room with two guys called Curtis and James and we all got on brilliantly. They were lovely lads and they reminded me a bit of myself at that age. They were really carefree and not thinking too much about the future. They were working very hard but they were also just having fun and taking each day as it came. That made my experience more enjoyable because they made me feel I should be more like them and not take it all too seriously.

The few days I spent at Bootcamp were quite brutal. It was hard work but there was also a lot of waiting around, and we sometimes felt like cattle being moved around from place to place. The downtime was good for getting to know people, and I ended up being really good mates with Adam and Jake, who also made it through to Judges' Houses. We spent a lot of time together and I'm still good mates with them now.

There was a bit of partying going on here and there, but I avoided all of that because I wanted to be right as rain to perform. It was like a whole new me, and it was hard walking through the lobby and seeing people drinking. The old me would have been straight in there with them all and I would have been last at the bar, but Bootcamp was far too important to jeopardise. I needed to be healthy and to put all of my energy into it to get the best results.

There were about three stages to get through, which meant several opportunities to get sent home. I had to sing both as part of a group and on my own, and out of all the guys who were there only six of us were going to make it, so the chances of me being one of them were tiny. I felt like I was really putting myself out there as a person and showing people who I really was, and I wasn't used to doing that. It wasn't something I was comfortable with, but it was the right time for me to do it. I'd spent a lot of my life being paranoid about who I was and I needed to start being proud instead. I felt as though getting through would make me feel I was worth something.

I sang alongside Curtis and James in the group performance. We all performed The Fray's 'How to Save a Life' and it was hard because it was a sing-off and they were both so good. None of us wanted to go home, of course, and they were my friends as well. The judges had total poker faces on while we were singing, so it was impossible to gauge their reaction, and when they put me through I was so pleased. I felt terrible for all the people who didn't make it, but I didn't have time to think about it too much because we went straight on to rehearsing our next song.

I sang Take That's 'A Million Love Songs' for my solo performance and I knew it was an interesting choice given that Gary Barlow was one of the judges, but I changed it around completely and tried to put my sound on it.

WHEN THE AUDIENCE AND JUDGES STOOD UP AND APPLAUDED AT THE END IT FELT TOTALLY UNBELIEVABLE.

When we all gathered to hear the final verdict I remember standing on stage staring at my tattoos and playing with my hands. I was doing anything to distract myself and calm my nerves. I had kind of prepared myself for going home and I felt very anxious about it.

I didn't have a proper plan B. I guess it was to go back to playing with the band and writing music, as I said, but I didn't want to go back to feeling the same despair as I had before.

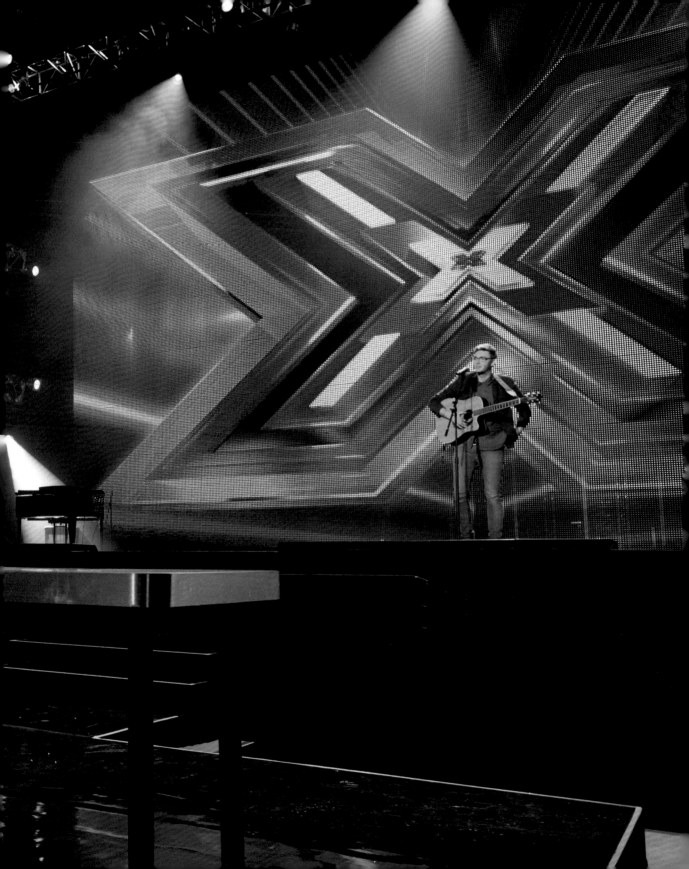

If I had been sent home I definitely would have thought about trying out for *The X Factor* again the following year. I like to think I would have taken a step back and looked to see how I could improve, to have a better chance of getting to the Live Shows. But if my self-esteem had crashed, I'm not sure I would have had the energy.

When my name was called and I realised I was through, it was the most incredible feeling. I guess I was ready for it. I was at the right point to put myself forward for something so big and take it on emotionally and mentally. Now it felt as if I'd got over another massive hurdle and I was on my way. I was so excited about going to Judges' Houses and having the opportunity to sing again.

I spent the month following Bootcamp being very thoughtful and anxious – I was kind of mulling over the fact that I was one round away from the Live Shows. I spent a lot of time on my own, thinking that I could change everything around and have a good life and be a more positive person. That was one of the longest months of my life and at times I felt I was going a bit crazy, but I changed quite a bit in a good way and I felt ready to take on Judges' Houses.

JUDGES' HOUSES

I had absolutely no idea where we were heading to for Judges' Houses, and I genuinely didn't care. Somewhere hot would have been lovely, but I was just happy to be there.

There were some rumours floating around here and there about where the Boys' category might be going, and who our mentor could potentially be, but I can honestly say that it was all a huge shock for me.

We all met at Heathrow airport and we were handed an envelope with details of where we were going. When I saw we were flying to Dubai I was so happy I thought I was going to be sick. It all felt like too much. It was somewhere I could only have dreamed about visiting, and now I was heading off on a flight with Adam and Jake, two guys I considered to be good mates. We had the same kind of musical tastes and similar outlooks on life, so it felt great that we were going through everything together. I also really liked Jahmene from the minute I met him. I thought he was adorable and so talented.

My audition was aired the same day we flew out, so it was a big day all round.

When we got to Dubai we were taken to this incredible villa. It was so posh it even had a bedroom for a member of staff, so they could look after you at all times. We didn't go for that, though, because we felt it would be a bit weird. It was already fancy enough.

We all bonded really well as a team of lads, and also with all of the crew who were out there with us. One night when we were having a few drinks around the pool, I looked over and Dermot was sitting there. It was so surreal. I remember thinking to myself, 'What is my life now? How did I get here?' The week before I'd been sitting at home feeling nervous and strumming on my guitar, and now I was having a beer and a chat with Dermot O'Leary.

Dermot is an amazing guy and he really takes the time to get to know the contestants. He doesn't just shoot in and out and do his bit on stage; he'll always make the effort to see how you're doing. He's one of the nicest people I've met throughout the competition.

I was so happy when I discovered that Nicole was my mentor because she'd liked me so much in my audition. When she came zooming up on a speedboat it was quite a moment. She's a worldwide superstar, so I was chuffed! Nicole is also one of the most beautiful women I've ever seen in my life.

I was a bit worried that we might have a language problem, with her being American and me being Northern. I literally thought that she might not be able to understand my accent. There can be a bit of an

English/American disconnect between people sometimes, so I was worried that she might not get me, but she was brilliant and we got along from the word go.

People may not know this about her, but she works so hard to make sure things are right.

SHE'D REALLY DONE HER HOME-WORK ON WHAT KIND OF ARTIST I WAS AND FIGURED ME OUT. SHE'S BEEN THE BEST MENTOR I COULD POSSIBLY HAVE ASKED FOR.

When Ne-Yo rolled up as well it was just ridiculous. He's an amazingly talented man, so to know he was going to hear me sing was mind-blowing.

I chose to sing Bonnie Raitt's 'You Love Me', and I was feeling incredibly nervous. At that moment I'd never wanted anything so much in my entire life. All I could do was wait, and hope that Nicole felt I'd done enough to go through to the Live Shows. It was a bit of a gamble, because I wasn't as obviously pop star-ish as some of the other guys.

ABOVE / Going to Dubai was amazing. Not only did we get to stay in an
incredibly posh villa, but also we all bonded really well as a group of lads.

I remember sitting outside in the sun before I went in to see Nicole, and thinking about how it could all end there. I desperately wanted it to continue. It was boiling hot and it all felt a bit like being on a knife-edge, because it was about to turn out to be either the best or the worst few days I'd ever had. I'd been convinced all day that I was going to be sent home.

Nicole called me in and she asked how I was feeling, and my answer was 'Terrified'. She said I was one of a kind and unique as an artist. She also said that I threw my heart and soul out there when I sing, and she's right – I get so lost in the moment. Then she echoed my fears that I wasn't right for the competition when she said she was concerned about whether the show was for me and whether I was strong enough to handle the industry. She could only take three of the six of us through, she said, and I knew how talented the other guys were – I thought that was me done.

It seemed to take literally forever for her to tell me whether I'd made it, then she looked at me and said, 'James, it's not good news ... it's freaking amazing news.' She was laughing her head off and I started jumping around. We had a hug and I laughed and said, 'I can't believe you did that to me!'

It was a really nice contrast of emotions. After thinking I was being sent packing it felt even better when she told me she was taking me through. Afterwards I had a chat with Dermot outside and I was totally buzzing. I said that I was over the moon and I felt complete, and I really, really did.

The first thing I did was call my family, and my mum was in tears.

After everything I'd put her through, to be able to make that phone call was beyond anything I'd ever imagined. Then I phoned my dad and he was going crazy. I did the same thing to them that Nicole had done to me, by starting off pretending it was bad news. I think they went through the same feelings as I did – a massive low followed by a massive high.

The flight home was quite tough, because we were travelling with all the other lads who didn't get put through to the Live Shows, and we'd shared the highs and lows of it all together. They were all really supportive, though, and I wish them all the luck in the world in the future. I'm sure we'll see some of them back on *The X Factor* again. I really hope we do.

I had about a month back at home before I was going to be moving up to London with all the other finalists. It was weird going back to normality after being surrounded by so much luxury, but it was good to get that reality check.

I celebrated getting through to the Live Shows with my friends and family, and then I started trying to get my head around the fact that I was going to be massively in the public eye. My audition had already been shown, so people were talking about me on Twitter and I was getting recognised sometimes when I was out – and I knew all that was about to be magnified by about a million.

I was in a bit of a state of shock about it all. There's no training for the sudden change – living your normal, everyday life one minute, and constantly being asked for your autograph the next – and I didn't know how well I'd handle it. But I was ready to take it all on.

ABOVE AND RIGHT / Nicole really messed with me before telling
me I'd got through to the Live Shows along with Rylan and Jahmene.

MOVING ON IN

Moving to London and seeing our hotel for the first time was amazing. In the space of a day I had gone from living in a bedsit to staying in a five-star hotel. Our rooms were massive and to be honest I've never seen anything like it. I felt overwhelmed that I was staying in such an incredible place. There was even a phone in the toilet. It was ridiculous. I was sharing with Rylan and when he first saw the room he screamed!

I'd packed loads of stuff because I didn't know how long I'd be away. It could have been only a week or two, or virtually until Christmas. I'd been living on my own for years, so I was fine about being away from home, but the whole lifestyle thing took some getting used to.

We had a few weeks to prepare before the Live Shows, which gave us a bit of time to get polished up, get to know each other and get used to being more in the spotlight. It was great getting to know the other guys. Of course I'd already met Rylan and Jahmene at Judges' Houses, and I think because we were all together so much everyone bonded really quickly and we became a proper team.

When it came to the makeover, I was honestly up for whatever they wanted to do to me. As I've said before, I was quite insecure about how I looked, so I wanted to improve myself. I'm aware that it's important to look good when you're in the public eye. I wanted to be the best I could, so I basically said they could do whatever they wanted – within reason!

To start with, the style team said that they wanted me to keep the Deirdre Barlow specs I wore, but I wanted a fresh start so I got contact lenses. I thought the glasses were a bit gimmicky. They are real glasses that I do actually need to see properly, but I didn't want to be defined by them. I had never been able to afford lenses before, so when I had the chance to get some, I took it.

Clothes-wise, not much changed – the labels in my clothes were just a bit better than usual.

I don't think I'll ever get used to people putting make-up on me because it's not something I've ever done, but it's all a part of the business and if that's what I need to do, then so be it. It was weird being made up for the first time, but I got used to it pretty quickly.

I was feeling happier by the day, but people around me probably didn't pick up on that too much because I'm not a big smiler. I find smiling very awkward generally, which made photo shoots interesting.

We had a lot of photo shoots that week, and I think I perfected the moody 'I'm a bit hacked off with my life' face – which I kept up throughout the rest of the series!

It was weird talking about myself when we had to do interviews. I kept thinking, 'Will anyone really be interested in this?' I totally embraced everything that was thrown at me and I saw it all as a positive stepping-stone to better things. I had no idea how much goes into making a show like *The X Factor*, so those first few weeks were a massive learning curve, but a really fun, interesting one.

RIGHT AND NEXT PAGE / I got to meet some amazing people during the competition, including Robbie Williams and Gwen Stefani. They were really supportive and gave me some great advice.

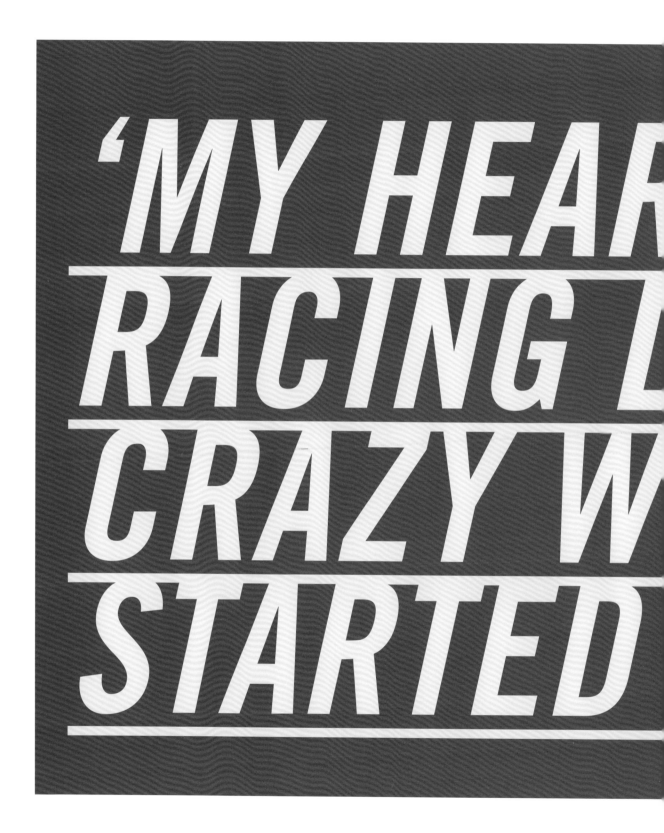
'MY HEAR
RACING L
CRAZY W
STARTED

WEEK 1

Theme: Heroes
Song choice: 'Stronger'

I wasn't overly confident with my song choice for Week 1 because it's not the kind of song I usually go for. I was pleased that they let me put a rap into it so I got to include my own lyrics. I don't think it was my strongest week, but overall for the first week I was pretty pleased.

The feedback was a bit mixed but mostly positive. Gary said he was worried I was losing a bit of my edginess and integrity and that I had to retain it. The crowd booed him and the other judges stuck up for me, but I totally valued his opinion. I guess the song was quite pop but I did try to put my sound onto it. I did stick up for myself as well and told Gary that I thought I'd made the song my own. It was important for me to have my own voice from day one.

Louis was very positive and said he thought I was going to go far in the industry and that I was different and original, while Tulisa said I was definitely a recording artist.

The first Sunday was so nerve-wracking. It's always stressful on a Sunday because you don't know who's going home.

WHEN YOU'RE IN THE X FACTOR BUBBLE IT'S HARD TO GET A GRASP ON WHO THE PUBLIC LIKES.

Of course no one wanted to go home any week, but Week 1 would have been the worst because you'd got all geared up and prepared for the competition and it would all feel like it was for nothing.

I felt terrible for Carolynne when she was eliminated. She'd been working towards that moment for a long time so it was especially hard to see her go home. I think whoever had gone in the first week would have had a hard time adjusting after the crazy few weeks we'd been through in the run-up to the first Live Show. Carolynne was really grounded and level-headed, so if anyone would have been able to deal with it, it was her.

RIGHT / It was pretty strange doing interviews and photo shoots and seeing myself in the papers, but I embraced everything that was thrown at me.

LEFT / I'd never had a makeover before, so it was a pretty weird experience, but it's all part of the business so I was honestly happy to let them do whatever they wanted – within reason!

WEEK 2

Theme: Love and heartbreak
Song choice: 'No More Drama'

I was really happy with my song choice in Week 2. Mind-bogglingly, Nicole actually arranged for me to speak to Mary J. Blige on the phone, which was a huge honour. Mary J. is an incredible artist and she was so nice to me. It was indescribable. I was feeling pretty confident about performing that week, but I think I put way too much pressure on myself and I felt quite panicky a lot of the time.

Nicole and I managed to take some time out to relax and we went to a pub together for a pint. I couldn't believe Nicole Scherzinger was eating pork scratchings! It's one of the best things I've ever seen.

My performance went okay, even though I was shaking before I went on. Once I started singing I felt a bit better and I gave it my all. The judges' comments were mind-blowing. Louis said I was a real artist with real talent and he complimented Nicole on the song choice. Tulisa picked up on the pain in my voice and said that she felt like every bit of drama in my life had been building up to that moment and she really believed what I was singing. Gary praised my technique and emotion and said it was a fantastic performance. Nicole was always so kind to me and she said I was on a whole other level.

WE BOTH GOT CHOKED UP WHEN SHE SAID I'D MADE MARY J. BLIGE PROUD THAT NIGHT BY COVERING HER SONG.

I left the stage feeling happy but a bit weird, and as soon as I got backstage I started feeling really unwell. I went dizzy and I started getting shooting pains up my arm. I had these really odd chest pains and I felt like I was having a heart attack or something.

I was really trying to keep myself calm but nothing seemed to help. An ambulance was called and I was checked out. It turned out to be a bad anxiety attack, and after I'd sat in the ambulance for quite a while they gave me the all-clear. The *X Factor* team looked after me really well that night and they got me back to the hotel so I could get some rest.

My name was called out first on the Sunday night, which was such a relief. If it had been one of the last I seriously think I might have ended up having another panic attack, because I still wasn't feeling great. I was sad that Melanie was sent home. She was like the mum of the group; she looked after us all and made sure we were okay. Obviously as she's a mum herself she's really empathetic and she was really missed by everyone.

I DIDN'T FEEL LIKE MYSELF FOR THE REST OF THAT WEEK.

Every time I stood up I felt as if I was going to have another panic attack, so I was constantly on edge, which didn't help matters. It was a horrible few days and I was grateful to have so many people around me keeping an eye on me and making sure I was okay.

This was love and heartbreak week, so it's the perfect time to talk about relationships. I'm single at the moment, and I guess that's a good thing because it's all so crazy right now, but given the choice I would rather be in a relationship. I would always rather be with someone than be single.

I'm a serial monogamist and die-hard romantic. I want a girl to look after me. Physically, I like brown eyes, belly button piercings and medium-sized boobs! On a mental level, I'm looking for someone who is kind, creative and funny. I wouldn't say I'm on the lookout for a relationship, though, because I don't think you should go looking for love. You should let it come to you.

I had a few snogs during the show, but I'm not going into details. We'll leave it at that. When this is all over, I fully intend to investigate some of the nice offers I've had …

I'm a proper romantic and when I'm with a girl I treat her really well. I'm very respectful and I like to look after whoever I'm with. I'm not going to lie – I have serenaded ladies I've been in love with before. Back in the day I used to write songs for girls when I liked them. It was my brilliant plan to get girls to like me.

MY GUITAR HAS SEEN ME THROUGH LOTS OF RELATIONSHIPS AND HELPED ME GET OVER HEARTBREAK MANY TIMES.

I definitely hope that one day I can settle down and get married and have kids, but I'm definitely not in a position to do that just yet. I think things will be busy for a while and I want to wait until I've got a bit of money behind me and I've got a stable home. Those are all things I'd like one day.

LEFT / Although I was happy with my live performance in Week 2, the panic attack I had when I came off stage made it a pretty stressful week.

WEEK 3

Theme: Club classics
Song choice: 'Sexy and I Know It'

Having just had a pretty tough week, I was glad that I felt really comfortable with my song choice in Week 3, having already performed it at Judges' Houses. That meant that even though I still had to work hard, I didn't feel stressed about it. I wanted to give the song some edge, so it had a bit of a Fatboy Slim sound, and it went really well. I loved being in the studio and routine-ing – which basically means working out how you're going to move on the stage – and although I wouldn't say I'm a natural mover, I learnt a lot about choreography. I can't imagine I'll ever be dancing around the stage doing full-on dance routines. It was great in terms of learning how to hold myself on stage though.

I was given some time to rest during the week to make sure my health was totally okay for the Saturday night. For the first time I had dancers all around me during my performance, so that was more pressure, but very good pressure. They were gorgeous! That was one of my favourite weeks by far.

RIGHT / My Week 3 performance of 'Sexy and I Know It' has to be one of my favourites by far. For the first time I had dancers all around me, and they were absolutely gorgeous!

Gary Barlow told me it was the performance of the series, which blew my mind. Louis commented that I was a professional and I deserved a record deal. Tulisa said it was an amazing rendition of the song and she loved that I'd had fun – and Nicole was as hilarious as ever, saying I had 'passion in my pants'. I honestly don't know where she gets her comments from. Dermot was taking the mickey out of me afterwards, saying that I 'nearly smiled'. How could I not with feedback like that?

I'm really into my urban music so I was a big fan of MK1 and I was gutted to see them go on the Sunday night. Of course as usual I was very happy to be staying, but it was tough seeing more and more people leave the competition. It was even weirder when bands left, because it meant that several people left the hotel and our group felt smaller and smaller.

My confidence was building and building as the weeks went by. My self-belief received a boost every time I got good feedback, or even if someone just came up to me when I was out and about and said that they liked my music. It made such a difference hearing nice comments, and it made me realise more and more that I was really good at what I did.

WEEK 4

Theme: Halloween
Song choice: 'Sweet Dreams (Are Made of This)'

The competition got more and more intense as each week went by, but I think that pushed us all to perform better than we ever had. I could see the other contestants improving each week, and while of course everyone wanted to win, we all supported each other, which was so nice. If ever anyone was feeling a bit rubbish you had this group of amazing people who would make you feel good again and remember why you were there. Rylan was literally always in a good mood. Even when things got tough he was smiling through it all, and he was great to talk to.

I got a real boost this week when I met and performed with Labrinth at one of his gigs in Manchester. How many people get to say they've done that? He was such a down-to-earth guy, and it's great meeting people who are doing so well but staying so grounded. To me he's the complete package, so it was a real honour and I was so grateful for his time. Just to be in the same room as him was surreal.

I also got to do a masterclass with Robbie Williams. That was incredible because he knows the business inside out and he gave me some great advice about staying true to myself. It was so crazy that I was meeting all of these amazing people that I've looked up to for so long.

I got really into my performance this time. I think people saw a real rock side of me. The production team went to town on the set and it was brilliant. The grim reapers and monks were well creepy! There was a really dark and sombre atmosphere in the studio. I was a bit disappointed with how my last chorus went because I thought I could've done better, but it happens. The adrenalin kicked in and I lost control of my vocals a bit. Maybe I can blame Nicole for looking so amazing? Her outfit was visually arresting. She's always stunning but she looked better than ever that night. People were always asking if I had a crush on Nicole, and I guess I do have a little one, purely in a professional way of course!

After I sang, Louis said he didn't think they'd had anyone like me on *The X Factor* before, and Tulisa said I'd made an old-school classic sound modern and she could see me in the final. Gary was also enthusiastic and commented that it was a performance that showed I wanted to win the competition. Of course Nicole threw in a funny comment, saying she thought the performance would give lots of girls sweet dreams.

I thought Jahmene was incredible that week singing 'Killing Me Softly'. Jade was eliminated this week, and I was really surprised because I thought she had one of the best voices in the competition. She's a lovely girl as well. There was no rhyme or reason about who ended up in the bottom two, so all I could do each week was hope that people voted for me.

RIGHT / I got really into this performance. The set design and the atmosphere were great and I think people got to see a real rock side of me.

LEFT / Sunday nights were always tough because it meant saying goodbye to someone – or several people – in the group. Of course we all wanted to win, but we all supported each other.

WEEK 5

Theme: Number ones
Song choice: 'Don't Speak'

It hit me in Week 5 that we were already around halfway through the competition and I couldn't imagine going back to my everyday life. You do find yourself getting totally caught up in everything, and because you're so busy time seems to fly by. I was going to clubs and being given free drinks, and hanging out with celebrities at parties … It wasn't like real life at all.

It helped seeing my friends and family each Saturday when they came to the show. That took me right back to my old life and kept me from getting too carried away with it all. I didn't always get a lot of time to see them, because there were always so many people backstage who wanted to chat, but I was always happy to talk to anyone who wanted to talk to me!

I certainly missed people when I was in the show, but you don't really have time to think about it.

The tiredness was the thing that got to me more than anything. We worked long hours and there were some mornings when I woke up and thought, 'I can't do another long day.' When this happened I'd give myself a talking to and remind myself how lucky I was to be there. A few months earlier I would have killed to be in a recording studio, and remembering that would get me through when I was fit to drop.

The good thing was we knew exactly how long we had to spend in the show and what we were working towards – it wasn't as if we were going to be working like that forever. Marvin from JLS actually said that our time in the competition would be the hardest we'd ever work, and if anyone knows, he does. I made sure I ate well and relaxed when I could. And if I'm being honest, no one forced me to go to the parties and things – that was my choice. I still loved every second of being there, and if tiredness was the worst thing that happened, I could deal with it!

Both Nicole and I loved my song choice that week. It's one of those songs that everyone knows and likes, so it was a bit of a gamble, but it paid off. I did a masterclass with No Doubt and it was amazing to meet them, but I felt slightly awkward singing their song back to them. It was so much pressure. I'm a big fan of theirs, and Gwen Stefani is smoking hot, so it was crazy to be doing their track while they stood and watched.

They laughed when I told them I was singing 'Don't Speak', and I think they thought I was a bit mad. My heart was racing like crazy when I started singing, but they were really nice about it and Gwen even said she'd watched some of my other performances. It was a bit of a dream come true to meet them.

Things went well on the Saturday night. Louis said that he loved the fact that I took chances with my song choices, and Tulisa said that I'd done something stripped back and relaxed and she felt like she was watching me at my own concert. Gary was as complimentary as ever, saying I always pulled it out of the bag and that he looked forward to seeing me each week.

NICOLE WAS LOOKING AMAZING THAT NIGHT, AND WHEN SHE SPOKE SO PASSIONATELY ABOUT ME IT MADE ME FEEL A BIT SHY.

It was horrible to see Kye go in the elimination. He's a top bloke and really talented. I know people were complaining about Rylan staying in every week, but he worked just as hard as everyone else and he entertained people, and that's why they loved him. I loved having him there. We all did.

WEEK 6

Theme: Best of British
Song choice: 'Hometown Glory'

It's always going to be a risk singing an Adele song, because it's impossible to better her, so I knew I had to do something totally different with it. I'd always said I would never cover an Adele song unless I could find a way to turn it right on its head. In the end we put a dubstep beat behind it to make it sound completely fresh and new. I don't think *The X Factor* had ever had someone doing dubstep before, so I was going out on a bit of a limb.

It's such an amazing song lyrically so it was fun to mess around with it. I started off doing an acoustic version, and then the beat kicked in and the atmosphere in the studio totally changed.

Louis said I was a brilliant interpreter of songs, which I think was my favourite comment of his so far. Tulisa called me credible, and Gary said that no one should ever cover Adele's song – except for me. Nicole said I 'swagged it' and called me the 'best of British'.

That night I thanked Nicole for all her help, because she had done so much for me week after week.

It was really upsetting to see District-3 sent home on the Sunday night when they were up against Union J – but I knew I was going to be sad to see either of them go, because we all got on well. District-3 and I used to have some good late-night harmony sessions where we'd sing along to Chris Brown songs. Ella and I wrote a few tracks together as well and I would love to work with her one day. I could never do a duet with Jahmene, though. He would totally out-riff me.

I was getting incredible support from celebrities during the show. Holly Willoughby, Chip (formally known as Chipmunk) and Niall from One Direction all tweeted amazing things about me. Professor Green also said he really liked what I was doing, and to get support from someone of his stature means so much.

He's phenomenally talented and really respected in the industry. I'd absolutely love to collaborate with him and write some music together. I really look up to him.

WEEK 7

Theme: Guilty pleasures
Song choice: 'Can't Take My Eyes Off You'

The Final was getting closer and closer and I think it was in Week 7 that it finally hit me how much I wanted it. I was having so much fun and I really wanted to make it all the way to the end.

We got invited to some amazing events while we were on the show. We went along to the premiere of the James Bond film *Skyfall*, which was incredible. I'd never been on a red carpet like that before and people were shouting our names! It was weird seeing all the stars like Daniel Craig there and people calling my name alongside theirs. It's what dreams are made of.

We also went to the Pride of Britain awards. That was a lovely event and I was so moved by the stories and the braveness of people. Things like that really put life in perspective for me, seeing how amazing the award-winners were. They were so deserving.

We also had a nice night out with Dermot one evening. He was worried that we were all cooped up in the hotel, so one evening he came by and took us all out for some drinks. It was a great way to chill out after some crazily busy days, and so thoughtful of him.

One of my best days was when we travelled to Disneyland Paris. We got recognised so much and it was crazy to think that people in another country knew who we were.

While we were there I rekindled my bromance with Rylan. He's just hilarious. He's taught me to see the light side of every situation. The energy there was magical and I fed off it. It must have been magical because it convinced me that wearing Mickey Mouse ear muffs and carrying a balloon was a good idea.

We all sang and it was the first performance I'd done in months that I wasn't being judged on. There's nothing like doing a live gig. It's where I feel most at home.

My Week 7 song wasn't my usual style of music but I really enjoyed performing it. Every week I tried to put my own twist on the tracks. This week I wanted to do something 'unplugged', so it was really back to basics.

Louis said the song was a bit safe but he liked it, and he thought I would get a record deal whatever happened. Tulisa said it was one of my coolest and most credible performances, even though it was guilty pleasures week. She also commented that it felt as if she was down in Camden listening to me in a club, which was well flattering.

LEFT / Being in the bottom two with Ella in Week 7 was horrible. She was like a sister to me throughout the competition and I was gutted when she got sent home.

Gary said, 'Putting my category aside – and I wouldn't normally say this – I want you to win this competition.' Nicole said I was mesmerising and inspiring. I was so humbled by the feedback. Comments would never fully sink in for me until after the show, so it was hard to react. I also felt really embarrassed at being flattered so much. I'm just not used to it.

It was pretty horrible being in the bottom two on the Sunday night, especially as I was up against Ella. I'm not the conventional *X Factor* contestant, so I wasn't surprised to find myself in the bottom two, but it still felt awful. I did a cover of the Alicia Keys song 'Fallin'', and that felt like I'd come full circle because I sang it at my first audition. I just hoped it would serve me as well. I really did put everything into it and felt every word.

Nicole and Gary both voted to save me, while Tulisa and Louis both chose to save Ella. That meant it went to the public vote, and when I found out I'd been saved I was incredibly grateful to everyone who had picked up the phone.

Ella, though, was like a sister to me and I thought the world of her, so I was absolutely gutted when she was sent home. I couldn't believe that she had been eliminated – I genuinely thought I was going home. I wanted to stay, of course, but never at the expense of someone like Ella.

I bounced back from being up for elimination pretty quickly, simply because I had to. People had voted for me and I didn't want to let them down by being a misery guts. I was in such a privileged position and I didn't take a second of it for granted.

WEEK 8

Theme: ABBA and Motown songs
Song choice: 'SOS' / 'Let's Get It On'

Seeing Ella leave the competition was such a shock – she's got the most amazing voice – and it made me want to work harder than ever, because I felt incredibly lucky to still be there. It seemed as if I'd been thrown a lifeline and I had to give everything I had – and then a little bit more on top. I kind of wanted to do it for Ella as well.

That week Nicole and I decided to look back through all my performances and see how much things had changed. It was very weird seeing myself performing Kelly Clarkson's 'Stronger', because it felt like years ago, although in fact it was only five or six weeks. It was mad. I remember that week so well because it was the first time I had the confidence to look into the camera rather than looking down or closing my eyes. It just showed me how far I'd come.

If anyone had ever told me I would be singing an ABBA song on stage in front of millions people one day, I would have laughed my head off. It was so far from anything I'd imagined myself doing.

I stripped it back and did an acoustic version because it felt like the right way to do the song justice.

I was nervous about the feedback because the track was out of my comfort zone, but actually it felt pretty good. Louis said he was glad I was still in the competition and he loved the way I merged angst and ABBA. Tulisa commented that I'd 'James Arthured' the track and predicted that even if I didn't win, I would sell more records than anyone else in the show. It was a lovely thing to say, but I don't know if it's something I believe. There were some amazing people there this year and I was in total awe of some of the performances.

Gary said he was glad I didn't conform and play it safe after being in the bottom two, and he said I'd got my integrity back. He was such a massive supporter of mine and it was hard to believe that someone so knowledgeable about music would rate me.

Nicole said I was a game changer and she commented on how hard I was working. To be fair, everyone was working hard! We all put the hours in, and I don't think anyone worked harder than anyone else.

I was more comfortable with my second song because everyone loves a bit of Motown. There were so many amazing Motown songs to choose from, but in the end we chose 'Let's Get It On' because it's such a great song and, again, I could take it back to being all about my voice and really show what I could do. I wore an amazing suit and I serenaded Nicole and Tulisa, so it was also a really fun performance for me. I could feel the love in the studio. I took a risk by being so raunchy!

138   **RIGHT** / I felt out of my comfort zone doing an ABBA song, but the judges
          seemed to like what I did with it. Tulisa said that I had 'James Arthured' the track.

Serenading Nicole and Tulisa in the way I did could have looked seriously tacky and cheesy, but I hope I styled it out. There's a fine line between being cheesy and making the song credible. It was a hard song to execute and I wanted to do it justice.

I would never have done anything like that back in the early weeks, so it showed how much more comfortable I was with being on stage in front of so many people.

Nicole was up dancing and there was such a great atmosphere in the studio. When I finished, Louis said it was the vocal performance of

ABOVE / Serenading Nicole and Tulisa with 'Let's Get It On' was risky, but I think it showed how much my confidence had grown during the competition, and in the end it went down well.

the night and that I was a world-class act. Tulisa said that only I could have gotten away with singing that song and that it was sexy and cheeky. Gary praised my vocals and said he didn't want people to compare me to other artists because I'm my own person – and Nicole said a lot of babies might be conceived that night because of my performance! She came out with some funny comments week after week and I loved it. The only thing I was gutted about that week was that I said the word 'woo' when I was talking about ladies in my VT for some reason. Then Dermot brought it up on stage. I have no idea why I used that word and I'll never use it again!

I was so sad to see Rylan go the following night. The bromance was over. He left on a high, though, and everyone loved him. We'd had such a laugh earlier in the week cooking a Thanksgiving dinner for Nicole – even if he did make me stuff the turkey.

I felt sorry for Rylan at times, because he was always blamed for other finalists being sent home. It wasn't his fault, and it's a testament to his character that he didn't snap and throw a hissy fit. He's a strong character and I think he's got a bright future ahead of him. He was missed by everyone in the competition when he went, and I cannot wait to see what he does next.

WEEK 9

Theme: Songs for you / Songs to get you to the Final
Song choices: 'One' / 'The Power of Love'

The attention was pretty intense in Week 9 and I don't think I'll ever get my head around the interest I get from girls. I've never seen myself as a heart-throb or anything like that. People were writing all this stuff about me and I was like, 'Really?'

I thought that week how weird it would feel to go back to singing in pubs after being on the show. I'd still treat it like I always have and put my all into it, but it would still feel strange after having sung to millions of people each week. With pub gigs you never know if people are coming to see you or if they just happen to be there having a drink, so you don't really know if they like you or not. When I perform now, people will be coming to see me because they know how I sound and they like it.

I was very pleased with both of my song choices for Week 9. We kept things really simple and it was just me singing – no guitar or dancers or anything.

'The Power of Love' is a big ballad and I hadn't done anything like that before. It was getting really near to Christmas and even though the song hasn't really got anything to do with Christmas it always reminds me of that time and it's a song that I love.

U2's track 'One' was dedicated to my sisters and my brother. I wanted to let them know through the song that I'm going to be there for them. I really want them to do well for themselves.

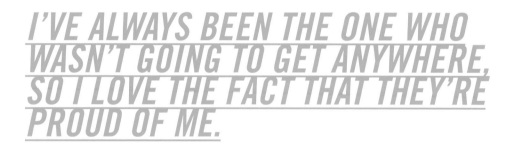

I'VE ALWAYS BEEN THE ONE WHO WASN'T GOING TO GET ANYWHERE, SO I LOVE THE FACT THAT THEY'RE PROUD OF ME.

And at the end of the day I had to get into the Final – all of my sisters said they'd already bought dresses to wear!

After I sang 'One', Louis said that every week I brought something new to the show and he thought I was going to have an amazing career. Tulisa said my performance was worthy of going through to the Final and I hoped she was right. She said that everyone assumed

I was going to get a record deal anyway, so they may not be voting, but she told me I deserved to win. Gary said I was like a lyrical boxer who came out and knocked the other contestants down one by one. He also said he'd be extremely disappointed if I wasn't in the Final in Manchester. Nicole was fighting my corner again and said I deserved to be in the final, but I had no idea if people wanted me there.

I was really panicking that I wasn't going to be in the Final. I really wanted to be there, because it was so close now and it would have been awful to miss out on the final week.

After my second performance Louis said that if there was any justice I would get through to the Final, and Tulisa said she felt so proud to be a part of the show because I'm on it. She'd said that before and I thought it was great. Gary said it was the performance of the series and that I make people feel emotional. Nicole commented that if I didn't get into the Final she didn't know what she was doing on the panel, and at that moment I welled up on stage because I just wasn't expecting such amazing comments at all.

I don't think I'd ever been as nervous as I was on that Sunday night. It was all down to the public vote, so I was praying they would support me. When my name got called out I just couldn't believe it. I was beyond happy ... I gave Nicole and Jahmene a hug and then took some deep breaths to calm myself down. I was in the Final!

LEFT / The judges' comments on Saturday night were amazing and   **149**
I got really emotional. When my name got called out on Sunday, I couldn't
believe I'd actually made it into the Final. It was an incredible moment.

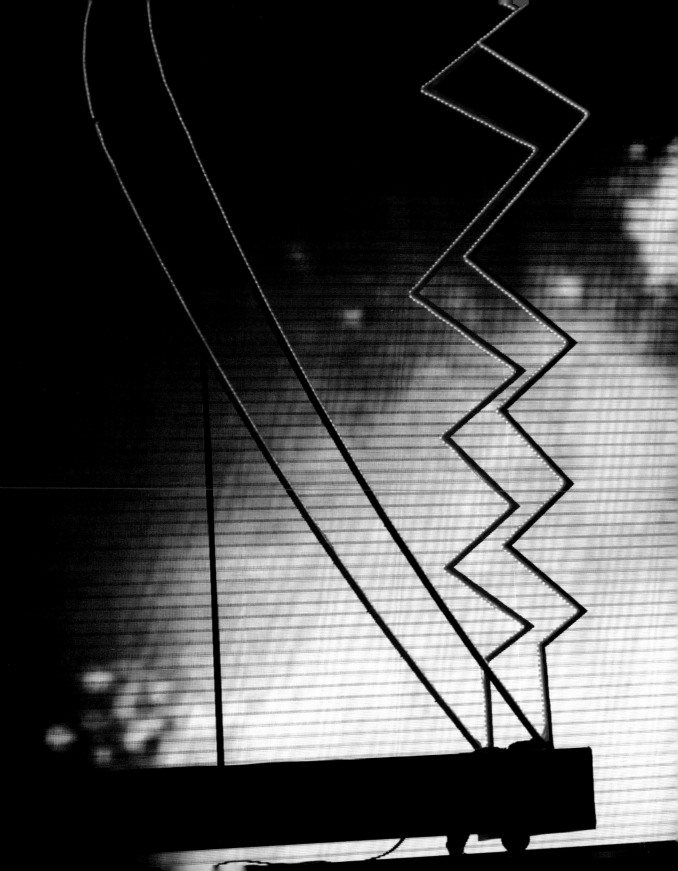

THE FINAL: SATURDAY

Theme: Big hits / Mentor duets
Song choices: 'Feeling Good' / 'Make You Feel My Love'

I was in the Final. It was amazing! We did such great things that week. One of the best was going to Downing Street to turn on the Christmas lights at Number 10 with David Cameron, and singing 'Silent Night' with Chris and Jahmene. I had to really take a step back and take everything in. That's not something you get to do every day.

Then there was homecoming, which included a gig, and the reception I got was amazing. When I arrived back home in Middlesbrough, the first stop was The Victoria pub in Saltsea, which I call The Vic. We came speeding up on motorbikes and Nicole was by my side, and I couldn't quite believe the size of the crowd. They had banners and they were chanting my name. I'd been hoping that a few people would turn out to see me, but there were so many! They're the ones I'd been doing all this for, so to know that they were supporting me meant everything.

It was great to be home, and I suddenly realised how much I'd been missing it. There really is no place like home. My mum and dad were there together, along with my siblings, and that meant so much. It was like one massive celebration.

We visited my old bedsit next, and I think that was a bit of an eye-opener for Nicole because it's so tiny. I felt really emotional being back there, because the period when I was living there was such a dark time for me. But here I was, with a totally different life and feeling like a different person.

I went on to perform my homecoming gig to an epic crowd. Nicole described it as 'James Arthur mania'. Being able to perform to my home crowd was the best feeling ever. They created an electric atmosphere and made me feel I could take on anything.

I wanted to win and I was prepared to fight for it. I was so honoured to be in Manchester for the Final. I was very nervous but ready for it. There were so many people there and I've never sung to such a massive crowd.

I really enjoyed singing 'Feeling Good', and the comments from the judges were incredible. Louis said the idea of *The X Factor* was to find someone new who could bring something different, and that was me. Tulisa said I was everything that the competition should represent in 2012 and that Britain should be proud of me. She also said I could take my music to America. Fingers crossed!

Gary commented that when I come onto the stage he becomes an audience member instead of a judge, and that it was my best

performance to date by far. Nicole said it was the start of a whole new life for me.

Before the show I'd sung for tiny crowds, and now I was in front of thousands of people, getting the most amazing feedback, and it felt wonderful. My local mayor was in the audience, which was so funny. And she said she thought I could win!

Singing 'Make You Feel My Love' with Nicole was indescribable. I loved it so much and she sounded amazing. Afterwards she spoke to Dermot about how far I'd come, but I knew a lot of it was down to her because she'd been such a brilliant mentor throughout. I had to thank her because she'd brought all of my confidence back.

Standing on the stage with Christopher and Jahmene while waiting to hear the verdict felt surreal. I was so nervous, because not to get to the Sunday night finale would have been such a massive letdown.

Dermot called Jahmene's name first and I was really happy for him. Then it was just between me and Christopher. I had absolutely no idea which way it would go, so when Dermot called my name I went crazy. I was shouting and pacing the stage, and then I gave Nicole a massive hug. I was through!

THE FINAL: SUNDAY

Theme: Song of the series / Winner's single
Song choices: 'Let's Get It On' / 'Impossible'

The Sunday of the Final was a mad day. It was so busy and hectic, but that was good because it made me forget my nerves to a certain extent. About an hour before the show started my nerves kicked in big time and I was pacing around trying to stay calm.

Jahmene and I walked on stage to 'Santa Claus is Coming to Town', which was a great way to kick things off.

We each had to choose a track we'd already sung during the series to sing again for our first performance. I chose 'Let's Get It On'. I had the most fun performing that the first time around. I loved hitting that high note and looking down and seeing Nicole dancing along. I didn't expect to get the reaction I got from it and I felt really overwhelmed that night. I was really hoping people would enjoy it as much again and pick up their phones and vote for me.

I enjoyed singing the song just as much this time around – if not a little bit more! Louis said that I was a real, credible and ready-made artist. He also told Nicole how amazing she'd been as a mentor, which I agreed with wholeheartedly.

Tulisa said that only I could take untouchable classics and make them my own, and that I deserved to win. Gary said I didn't need developing by a record label because I was there already, and he also admitted that he would download my album!

Nicole said she felt like she was seeing the future and that I could be back on that stage in a year's time performing. She also said she felt blessed to have been able to work with me, but I'd say I was the one who was blessed to work with her.

I couldn't believe how far I'd come since Week 1, and I also couldn't help feeling the whole thing was a dream and I was going to wake up!

After I'd sung my winner's song, 'Impossible', for my second performance, both Louis and Tulisa said they thought the competition was going to change my life.

Tulisa also said she thought that she and I were similar people, and that I'd fought my way out of the depths and come back with true 'heart'. Gary's comments were amazing. He said I had come to the competition as a true artist and that he had been worried that I'd lose some of my credibility trying to win votes! He went on to say that he was so proud I was on that stage, and that I mustn't ever let anyone tell me what to do when it came to my music.

Nicole told me I made her feel like anything is possible, and at that moment I felt the same way. I'd done everything I could. All I could do was wait and hear the results of the public vote.

My family and friends were in the audience and my mum said how proud she was, which really touched me. All of my friends had come dressed as me, which was hilarious. They were wearing caps and tattoo sleeves and carrying blow-up guitars. A video of my friends and family was also shown, and when they were saying how much they loved me I had to really hold back the tears.

I don't think I've ever experienced anything like the feeling I had when I was standing on the stage with Nicole and Jahmene waiting to hear the result. It was a mixture of excitement, nerves and complete and utter fear.

When Dermot read my name out it didn't feel real at first. I was so stunned. The audience were screaming my name, and when I looked around I thought, 'I've actually done it – I have won *The X Factor*.'

Dermot came over to speak to me, but all I could say was 'Thank you'. There were so many other things I wanted to say, but I was shaking and I couldn't get the words out. This kind of thing doesn't happen to people like me!

I felt bad for Jahmene at that moment, because I adore him, but I know he's going to have the most incredible career. He is ridiculously talented. I know he was happy for me because he told me so afterwards, which meant so much.

When Dermot showed me my single, it properly kicked in that I had just won *The X Factor*. I felt extra happy knowing that the profits were going to such an amazing charity, Together for Short Lives.

I then got to sing the winner's song again, and suddenly near the end all of the other finalists came running out from backstage and bundled me. Nicole came up and gave me a hug and I looked out into the audience and took it all in. I couldn't wait to go and celebrate with my friends and family. What. A. Night.

I AM IN TOTAL SHOCK. I STILL CAN'T BELIEVE I'VE WON!

I'd like to say thank you to all my family, especially my mum, dad, my sisters and my brother, plus all my friends, particularly my best mate Michael Dawson and Lucy Poole and her family, Andy, Janet and Jenny for all their amazing support.

I'd also like to thank *The X Factor* production team: all of the researchers (Joseph, Arlanda, Sarah, Ciara, Richard, Nathan and Kinvara), the APs, the runners, the make-up and hair team, the stylists, Tamsin Dodgson, Beth Hart, Mark Sidaway; special thanks to Rob Davies and Phil Myers, the press team (Russell, Caren, Emily, Grace, Justin, Nick and Ben) and basically everyone who worked on the show, because they were all amazing. I also want to say a special thank you to Emma Cassen for looking after me when I had my panic

attack. And a big thank you to Graham Stack, Simon Gavin, Matthew Rumbold, Ian James, Annie Williamson, Roz Colls, Caroline Killoury and Quest. And thank you Jake Quickenden and Adam Burridge for making Dubai so much fun.

Looking back, I enjoyed all of my performances, but I guess the highlights were 'Sexy and I Know It' and 'Hometown Glory'. I also really enjoyed 'Let's Get It On' and 'No More Drama'. Those are the ones that will always stand out in my mind. And, of course, the songs I did in the Final.

When I spoke to Mary J. Blige she told me to sing like I didn't have a choice and like I wanted to change something in my life, and now I always feel like I'm singing for survival. People seem to connect with me when I do that, so I know that I always have to give that level of performance. I always want to do my best, to say thank you everyone who's been behind me from day one.

I'm taking such amazing memories away from the show. Coming back stronger the week after I had my panic attack felt amazing, and getting through the first ever audition was quite a moment. I also loved our night out with Dermot, and Rylan's birthday party was great fun. I've been so lucky.

People have been so nice to me when I've been out. At first I found it quite daunting being recognised, but I'm getting used to it and I think it's helped me to be more outgoing around people I don't know. I also don't think anything will faze me after being on the show, because it's such hard work. I've learnt that I can keep my feet on the ground in the most stressful situations, so I'm really grateful for that.

Being on the show has boosted my confidence generally and increased my sense of self-worth. It's also reinforced my belief that my purpose will always be to do music, and that in turn has made me a more rounded person.

It feels like I've been working towards this moment for a million years, and that all the hard work I've put in has paid off. I know it sounds like a cliché, but this is my dream and it was starting to feel like it was never going to happen. I expected to do a lot more with my music earlier on in life and I almost gave up on the idea of it ever working out.

I told myself that if nothing happened with my music by the time I was 25, I would give it all up and get a proper job, and keep music as a hobby, so this has definitely come at the right moment. Winning *The X Factor* has given me the ultimate sense of achievement. It feels incredible to know that my life is going to be so, so different from now on.

Rylan and all of the other contestants helped to make being in the show a great experience. I was so lucky to be with such brilliant people. Also big thanks to the James Arthur Band and, of course, the Jarmy, who have been incredible. I wouldn't be here without them.

Finally, I want to say a huge thank you to Nicole, Gary, Tulisa and Louis for giving me such great comments. Obviously I want to say an extra special thank you to Nicole. She's a real muso and she did her background work on me. She listened to all of the other music I'd done over the years and she figured out who I was and how I worked. She's been positive and honest with me throughout the show. She's been the ultimate mentor, and my winning is to her credit. She's Sha-mazing!

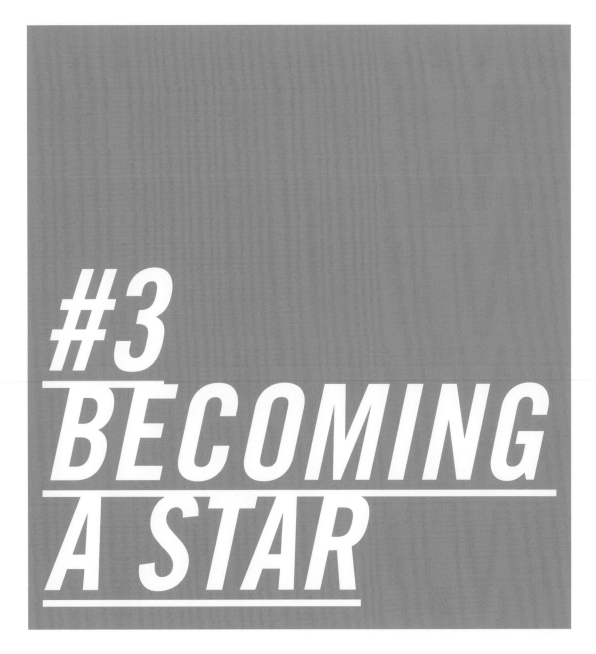

#3
BECOMING
A STAR

THE FUTURE

I'm so excited about the future. I would love to have triple-platinum-selling albums and to still be making music for the masses in ten years' time. I'd also love to venture into some British films and do some acting, and maybe even write and produce songs for other people. I want to help the UK music scene as much as I can.

Breaking America is another massive goal of mine. That would be fantastic. I've got the platform now, and it's incredible to be given this opportunity.

On a more personal level, *The X Factor* definitely made me feel better about everything. It gave me the hope that I could have a nicer lifestyle and be able to afford my own place and help my family out one day. Even though my life is much busier and more hectic now, I feel more settled within myself than I ever have before. I learnt so much about myself during the competition, and also about music and performing. It was like a crash course in the music industry and I loved every minute of it.

It's crazy to think that of all those people who auditioned for *The X Factor*, I've won. Now everything I've ever wanted is within reach. I'm totally reinvigorated as a person and I feel complete. Thank you again for all your incredible support throughout the whole thing. I can't wait to get started on my debut album!

HarperCollins*Publishers*
77-85 Fulham Palace Road,
Hammersmith, London W6 8JB

www.harpercollins.co.uk

First published by HarperCollins*Publishers* 2012

1

James Arthur is represented exclusively by Quest Management (UK) Ltd.

The X Factor is a trademark of FremantleMedia Ltd and Simco Ltd.
Licensed by FremantleMedia Enterprises www.fremantlemedia.com

Principal photography © Ken McKay
Personal photographs on pp 14, 16, 21, 24 and 27 courtesy of the author

Photograph on p.21 © Hubb Photography

A catalogue record of this book is available from the British Library

ISBN 978-0-00-742672-0
Ebook ISBN 978-0-00-749026-4

Printed and bound in Great Britain by Butler Tanner and Dennis Ltd, Frome, Somerset